# FEAR OF FORKS

BY THE SAME AUTHOR

Full collections:

*Red Devon* (Seren, 2013)
*Berg* (Seren, 2009)

Pamphlets:

*Human Tissue* (Smith|Doorstop, 2020)
*Wheelbarrow Farm* (Templar, 2010)
*Extra Maths* (Smith|Doorstop, 2005)

ACKNOWLEDGEMENTS

Thanks to editors of the following publications, in which some of these poems previously appeared: *Acumen, Southword Literary Journal.*

'Hallmark' was shortlisted for the Plough Poetry Prize (as 'Hallmarked Birmingham, 1934'); 'Living Donor' was commended in the 2021 Hippocrates Prize (as 'Donor').

Thanks to Andy Brodie, my husband and partner in crime at *The Friday Poem*, and to Charlotte Gann, Khadija Rouf and Steven Lovatt for fine criticism and blunt encouragement.

Thanks also to artist Rachel Ross for permission to use her beautiful painting of pickle forks on the jacket [https://www.rachelross.co.uk]

First published in 2022 by Happen*Stance* Press
21 Hatton Green, Glenrothes KY7 4SD
https://happenstancepress.com
ISBN: 978-1-910131-72-5



Printed & bound by Imprint Digital, Exeter
https://digital.imprint.co.uk

Chris, hello!
Hilary x

# FEAR OF FORKS

*Hilary Menos*

Hilary Menos

HAPPENSTANCE PRESS

# Contents

## PICKLE FORKS

Today we are going to polish the family silver—
this bosun's whistle, my grandma's antique salver,
your nan's salt cauldron with the frilled edge,
my auntie's pepper pot with its jaunty grin,
her matching mustard dish with blue glass lining,
the napkin rings from your dad's Masonic lodge
and these scuffed cases of cutlery, eBay's finest—
second-hand, some monogrammed, distressed—
bought in the first flush of making a home.

Some we use—the cake tongs, the oyster forks,
the shovel-shaped caddy spoon, the fancy carver,
three tiny salt spoons in a vintage matchbox.
Some others, never—cutlery rests, a fish server,
six butter knives with handles of malachite green,
the deco coffee spoons, each with its Bakelite bean.
And lastly, and most loved, these pickle forks—
my four small princes with their spiky crowns
and handles of silver, mother-of-pearl and bone.

## AUCTION

Here I am, again, in these auction rooms
browsing the silverware section for old spoons.

Jam spoons, salt spoons, teaspoons with wrythen knops
(a mint boxed set complete with sugar nips),

a George III, shell-bowled sauce ladle,
a silver christening spoon with nail-head finial,

a dozen apostle spoons, each saint with his emblem
finely wrought at the tip of a grooved stem,

even *repoussé* berry spoons—Victorian bling—
each one a perfect treasure. All these darlings

laid out like pale corpses on velvet or silk
or rubber-banded tightly, shank to shank,

begging me to buy them, no matter how dear,
and tuck them up at home in my cutlery drawer.

## LIFELINE

The waxed canvas smell of this jacket, new at the time,
transports us back to that Friday night in *Urgences*
where we sat either side of our boy, his small fist
bandaged, waiting for the next available nurse

and—to distract and amuse him—played *Lifeline*,
an interactive mobile phone game where Taylor
is stranded on a space station on the moon
and needs our help to find his way back home.

Should he venture outside to fix the air supply unit
using the only oxygen tank, the last length of frayed rope?
We talk it through while medics come and go
asking again about the thumb and the whittling knife

and wait while the game applies choice and algorithms.
Should he descend into the crater or go round?
Is he navigating the air lock, scaling the hull
or flailing in space at the end of an untethered line?

A decision is made: the tendon needs surgery now.
Again we wait—and now you tell me, quietly, urgently,
about finding him in the field, the amount of blood,
how he'd tried to staunch the flow with grass

—until at last he's wheeled back in to us, shiny-eyed,
and we sit in that sunlit room on the Children's Ward
and play *Lifeline* until we manage to rescue Taylor
or they discharge us, whichever comes first.

## HALLMARK

A double row of round bowls, sextuplets
top to tail on a bed of black velvet;
each one a teardrop, a rigid balloon,
a quail's egg on a stick, a puppet moon.

So many spoons, cupped hands made manifest:
King's pattern, Queen's pattern, kept cased for best
or tarnished, rolling in drawers, handles loose,
dark with age or the patina of use.

Faces open to the sky, they fill, brim,
tremble with liquid light the day pours in.
Look closer and see the whole room, your face
distorted, upside down and obvious.

## RACK, FROM LEFT

His birthday Petty, his Christmas sharpening steel,
the Kitchen Devil with melted plastic butt and no style,

the oyster shucker with blue hilt (£10 from Amazon)
that outperforms our Blenheim Forge Limited Edition,

the chef's knife made of local Gresigne oak
which he sawed and riveted onto an old knife blank,

his orange fishing knife with shackle key and spike,
the palette knife I've used to ice every birthday cake,

the ornate Christofle carver bought from *Le Bon Coin*,
the whittling knife which did all that damage to his thumb

and last, his Gorse Nakiri with a handle of buffalo horn
and a blade shaped like a sperm whale,
                                        its Damascus pattern

like contour lines on a map. With these tools to hand
our son is fit for this, and that, and any other world.

## KNIFEWORK

This week his homework is knife cuts.
He waits at the block in full whites, apron and *toque*,
a carrot in one hand, his new chef's knife in the other.
Beside him, a head of celery, a bundle of leeks
and a red net of onions. I feel a *mirepoix* coming on.

He starts with strip cuts—*pont-neuf* (perfect for chips),
*battonets, alumettes, juliennes*. He slices, shreds,
measures and minces, until the board is covered
with stacks of sticks and a shower of *chiffonade*.
Then on to the cube cuts, in descending order—

*carré, parmentier, macédoine, brunoise fin*.
Behind him, on the beech rack, his first knife,
the Petty we had made for his tenth birthday
with an A1 steel blade, a handle of lignum vitae
and a ferrule forged from a brass threepenny bit.

He peels and turns and weighs the last of the spuds
—*château* (like a rugby ball), *à l'anglaise* (like an egg)—
slides them into a pan, wipes his knife clean
and puts it back in his standard-issue plastic *mallette*
with the whisks and the ladles and the spoons,

the brushes, ballers, sieves, tweezers, spatulas—
all the tools of his trade, the means
to prise open, pare, fillet, get close to the bone,
prep and plate up, working with broad strokes and fine
and with so much craft it starts to seem like art.

## JOE

He's doing an unboxing video for his YouTube channel.
I'm holding his phone while he chats to camera,
slits the packing tape, prises open the cardboard carton
and shows each item to the screen for two seconds exactly.
Catalogue. Manual. Rainbow stickers. Grey felt mat.
The weighty steel barrel of his new burr grinder.

Makes me think back to the year of homeschooling,
the lesson plan he devised for himself aged fourteen
scrawled in green felt-tip pen on squared paper—
a curriculum of coffee. History, geography, politics,
the mathematics of extraction yield, the art of the barista,
pottery workshops making glazed espresso cups,

and science—water as a universal solvent,
the effect of caffeine, the chemistry of caramelisation,
the physics of particle size, grinding, extraction,
kettle streams and turbulence and agitation,
—how to release volatiles trapped in the coffee matrix,
to find the ultimate sweet spot between sour and bitter.

On his bedroom wall not Spiderman or *Stranger Things*
but a poster of the coffee taster's flavour wheel—
a kaleidoscopic burst of pink and red and green and blue,
a sensory lexicon, the universal language of coffee
with flavours from ash to wood, from peapod to pipe tobacco
—all the words you need for the perfect cup of joe.

## FLUXX

Sunday morning. Family time. *Zombie Fluxx.*
We've had eggs and coffee, and now more coffee.
We need a lot of coffee to play *Zombie Fluxx*, doughnuts too,
and a chainsaw and a baseball bat and a shotgun.
And a car and gasoline and a piece of four by two.

I've got most zombie cards on the table so I'm Zombie Boss.
I have the zombie quartet, a trio and some singles—
Zombie Ballerina, Zombie Dinner Lady and Zombie Scientist.
When we pick up a zombie card we have to moan
so there's been a lot of moaning from my side of the table.

Outside, the sunflowers have dried to the colour of mud
and their heads, heavy with seeds, hang down.
When the wind kicks up, it rustles their crumpled foliage
and makes them lurch. We're talking about toilet paper,
how much we would need to stockpile in a zombie apocalypse.

It depends on the number of sheets in the roll, you say.
It depends on the thickness of each sheet, I say.
We discuss bidets, and newspaper, and dock leaves, in that order,
how Australian supermarkets are running out of toilet paper,
how people are bulk buying, how Australia is ramping up

toilet paper production due to the panic—
which is odd, I say, as they've only got eighteen cases
in the whole country. No, twenty-six, you say
you read in the paper yesterday, so we check
and it's a hundred and twelve.

## GOÛTE SEL

I had a bare life under your tread
floundering in salt marshes, my
soul bottled and corked, my
body thin on a diet of dull bread

until I sucked salt
out of the air, heard
salt cracking in the fire, felt
salt rough under my feet.

I mixed cornmeal with wood ash and
                    wove my pattern on the floor
a central line for the spirits, a snake in coils,
a sabre, a checkerboard heart and
                    wide symmetrical curls,
three starbursts and an open corner

where I slipped out, leaving you guessing
and as I left, poured salt over my own trail
took my broom and swept myself
out of my own home.

## DARYL DIXON IN THE VEGETABLE GARDEN

I'm digging spuds and suddenly he's there in the field
just yards away, his crossbow hooked casually over his shoulder
looking (frankly) rough as fuck. He nods to me silently
then climbs up onto the roof of the old well and sits
scanning the horizon for zombies and whittling a stick.

The asparagus crowns fascinate him. He picks one up
and put it on his head. 'King Asparagus,' he says with a grin
and starts dancing and prancing about in his redneck way.
I just sit back on my heels and watch. I can't believe it.
Daryl Dixon, dancing, in my vegetable garden.

After that he's there every day. I show him how to train
gherkins up a wigwam frame, pinch out gourds, dib in leeks.
He makes his rows tidy and puddles them in with care.
Sometimes he leans his crossbow against the wheelbarrow
and I stand guard for him, he's so absorbed.

We don't talk much. I ask him about the zombies once.
'Sometimes people see zombies where there aren't any,' he says,
'and sometimes people don't see the zombies at their door
because they've been there all their lives.'
I have no idea what he meant.

I can see him now, lying in the shade of the plum tree
between the kale and the lettuce, eating peas from the pod,
his leather vest with angel wings draped over a currant bush.
He stays until you come out to call me for supper
with the world tightly wrapped around your face.

## RED DRESS

Our first post-lockdown outing is for a funeral collation.
We're driving into town wearing proper clothes.
The boy is in the back seat watching a YouTube video
that says metal has memory because it springs back into shape.
That's not memory, I say, they're confusing terms,

a piece of metal would be rubbish at *The Generation Game*
where you have to remember what's on the conveyor belt
—the blender, the dinner service, the cuddly toy—
him sweaty in his tight suit, her in a frothy crimplene frock,
Bruce Forsyth gurning, Anthea twirling in chiffon

and the studio audience hollering *Blender! Cuddly toy!*
And it nearly wasn't a microwave or a foot spa or a fondue set
for the winner but a fistful of BBC licence fee stamps
which (left at the lights) leads us to zombie memory.
Do they repeat behaviours from their old lives

like the shopping zombies in *Dawn of the Dead*
or Morgan's wife in *The Walking Dead Series One*
loitering in her front garden, clutching her doorknob,
peering through the peephole in her old front door?
The boy says no, that's not in the comics at all, zombies don't

have memory because memory is what makes us human,
see? And we struggle out into the forty degree heat
and walk up the long tree-lined drive to Michael's house,
which was where we last saw Izabelle, just before lockdown,
dancing carefully in her best red dress.

## DÉSESPOIR DES SINGES

First time we drive to school after last week's storm
the trees that were down have been shifted, sawn, stacked.
A council crew pile the last of the fallen branches into a pick-up
—they are friendly, laughing, able—and I'm reassured again
at how this works. How we seem to manage chaos.

But that night, the wind ripping tiles off roofs, the furious rain,
all of us leaping out to drag branches out of the road,
our way blocked, turning back three times, nosing home on tracks
through the fields, thunder, lightning, all of us soaking wet
and me (at least) thinking how easy it is to die.

Now the sky is blue and the boy tells me his video game
has dragons whose magic scales keep them alive
though the one without scales called (obviously) Seath the scaleless,
is different. We're all different, I say, thinking of my boys
and the various ways they deal with things, or don't

and because yesterday was Mothers' Day and my new jasmine
is on the kitchen table waiting to be planted out,
I remember the monkey puzzle cutting, taken and potted up
by the boy who—in between all that business with kidneys—
spent a year in overalls learning to help things grow.

It was barely a foot high, bedded in peat, with leaves
like scales and a tiny, spiny trunk. Just one slim branch.
We tried to transplant it into a different soil, and it took at first.
Here they call it *Désespoir des Singes*—Monkey's Despair.
It didn't survive, and it's almost too much to bear.

## LIVING DONOR

I feel like a debutante at my first ball. My gown
is a simple wraparound number, slightly worn,
with hand-tied bows. Every face is on me.
I smile nervously, and examine my dance card
*—polka, lancers, two-step, waltz, quadrille—*
every space on my card has been filled by Mr Kadi.

I have a bracelet on each wrist but no other jewellery
and as I go in they offer me a mask.
Everyone's wearing one. It's a masked ball!
And there's Mr Kadi waiting for me, also in a mask
and a funny little hat and a green suit—
rather ill-fitting, I think, but I don't say so.

Things blur. Did someone spike my drink?
I seem to have lost my slippers, my white kid gloves.
The ushers have draped me in blue garments
with a peekaboo gap at the midriff. Above us,
the lights are five-petalled flowers, or an alien plant.
Mr Kadi takes me in his smooth, clean hands

*—plié, écarté, cambré, tendu, révérence—*
and the dance we do owes something to ballet,
something to autopsy, something to love.

## FEAR OF FORKS

fear of photographs of forks, pictures of forks
        3D forks in clay or wax or plaster
of brown Play-Doh prongs rammed on the end of a pencil
        the buckle and snap of polystyrene tines
the futility of a *papier mâché* utensil

fear of flatware, of fine dining, of dining etiquette
        of not knowing (or not following) the outside-in rule
fear of being an outsider, of being found out
        of being shown to have no manners or (worse)
                to have 'American' style

fear of forked lightning, of things branching, of trees
        of diagrams, divergence, any swift moving apart
fear of splay, sprawl, splits, of mental gymnastics
        the brain heading one way,
                and the heart ...

fear of forks in the road, of crossroads, crosswords, clues
        —1 ACROSS, a bifurcation (4)
fear of the road disappearing into the dark
        fear of over-specialisation—
the pickle fork, the spaghetti fork, the two-tined snail fork

fear of being pulled in two directions at once
        of chasing two hares in a field and catching none
of being neither fish nor fowl nor good red herring
        like that most poignant of hybrids
                the spork

## UNIVERSAL KEY

When she comes to stay, she brings a clock.
It has a mahogany case decorated with fruit wood inlay,
four brass balls for feet, and a universal key.

She winds it and sets it going, closes its small brass door
with a click. Together we stand, look, listen.
Its neat tick counterpoints my messy kitchen.

I put it on the mantelpiece, wind it once a week
—a sacred ritual for my temporal life—
or it stops and no amount of winding can start it,

or it stops and I don't care and the key gets lost
and the clock is deposed, relegated to a high shelf.
Or I drop it off a cliff. (There are many versions.)

She leaves at warp speed on a journey to find herself
and I go on mine, each of us with our own trajectory.
Now, when we meet, we're misaligned

but neither can agree on who has run on ahead
and who has fallen behind. We seek safe territory,
each keep to our side of the wrong conversation.

Inside the mahogany carcass the brass pendulum
swings to and fro—thesis, antithesis, thesis.
I wish we could be how we were back then.

The face has a painted garland of pink roses.
This clock is losing time. I open the glass front,
re-set the hands. I already know what will happen.

## SELF PORTRAIT

In *Still Life With Lemons and Game Fowl*
am I the bowl
or am I the bird
with ruffled ochre feathers and lolling head

or am I one of the lemons
the one at the bottom of the bowl under all the other lemons
unseen
weight-bearing

or am I the painter in his seventeenth-century garret
appraising this incongruous collection of objects
adding a smear of Dutch orange
for that trendy sepia look

or the painter's wife
bending over the domestic accounts in her alcove
counting her linens
raising a painterly eyebrow at the price of lemons?

## LA DIABOLICA FORCHETTA

She brought a fork to her wedding feast.
The prongs are the devil's horns, says the priest,
the fork is an agent of slackness and perversion—
it reveals the debased ways of the East
and corrupts our plain and decent Western women.

He lambasts her luxurious Byzantine silks,
her perfumed rainwater baths, her eunuchs—
but mostly the golden fork in its silver case. He says
God in His wisdom has given us natural forks
and waggles his filthy fingers in her face.

## WHAT EVERY WOMAN NEEDS

For the price of a small car, this can be mine—
a solid silver, 78-piece, Georg Jensen canteen
in the famous Acorn pattern. I stroke one fork.
Its decorative ferrule echoes the scrolls
at the end of the ridged stem. I linger, examine
the stylised motif. Part bee, part pineapple.

It's a classic set, he says—just the essentials—
all I need to bring elegance to my dining room
in a sturdy wooden trunk with a lift-out tray
and brass carrying handles (though sadly no key).

Or something to better suit my lifestyle, he flatters,
—a caviar shovel, oyster forks, lobster picks—
because what every successful woman needs
is a boxed set of Art Deco cocktail sticks.

| | |
|---|---|
| Table knives | 8000 |
| Dinner forks | 8000 |
| Butter knives | 400 |
| Fish forks | 1500 |
| | |
| Dessert spoons | 3000 |
| Egg spoons | 2000 |
| Salt spoons | 1500 |
| Mustard spoons | 1500 |
| | |
| Grape scissors | 100 |
| Oyster forks | 1000 |
| Asparagus tongs | 400 |
| Sugar tongs | 400 |
| | |
| Fruit forks | 1500 |
| Tea spoons | 6000 |
| Toast racks | 400 |
| Lifeboats | 20 |

## MIS EN PLACE

After a year on the Bac Pro Cuisine
he is au fait with the *mise en place*, blasé with a baton,
each polished knife, fork, spoon

nudged by a knuckle to an inch from the table edge,
glasses for water, white wine, red, triangulated,
salt cellar facing the kitchen.

As skilled as the seventeen assistant waiters
—Italian, French, Spanish, Swiss—
who landed a job with Cunard's White Star Line

(two guineas a month for the voyage)
in Gatti's fancy restaurant nicknamed 'The Ritz',
posher even than the first-class dining saloon.

They slept four to a cabin on E-deck
—Battista Allaria, the Peracchio brothers, Minio Zanetti—
played tag, shared stories of home

until the night when everything slid
and the soup spoons for Consommé Olga,
the dinner knives for Roast Squab,

dessert spoons for Peaches in Jelly and Waldorf Pudding
and all the butter spreaders and gravy ladles,
the oyster forks, asparagus tongs, grape scissors,

tea spoons, coffee spoons, salt spoons—the entire
canteen—were sucked into the depths,
spangling like silver fish all the way down.

## CHOP BOY

When I see him slicing *boudin noir*
or shucking oysters with the men
or teasing apart an urchin's inky spines
to reach the sweet salt centre

I remember his first *andouillette,*
his first *steak tartare,*
his first plate of *tête de veau,*
the pigs' ears in that shady Basque bar

and before that, a chop in each fist
up to his elbows in pesto,
grinning red jelly from ear to ear
the first crisp, the first ripe grape

and before that, before the mediation
of knives, forks, spoons, even before hands—
when he was all palate and throat
all belly and bliss.

## SPŌN

We go into the green wood, the big man and me
and walk until we feel the weight of a felled tree
or find a piece of dead standing timber
or a fallen branch hanging.

A spoon is a bowl with a handle asking to be held;
it requires cuts both measured and instinctive.
The big man dreams of carving a thousand spoons
from a single tree

and I am learning to embrace chaos,
each bend in the grain. A knot
is a break in the current I must learn to flow around,
there's no straight line, no sure end.

We sit among the chips, the shavings and splinters,
paring and polishing until we're both done.
There is his spoon. Here is mine.
Both are the product of rough work, and fine.